Communion
Connection
Giving
Sharing
Insight
Revelation
Solitude
Empathy
Understanding
Determination
Trust
Preservation

PERSONAL INFORMATION

NAME

SURNAME

ADDRESS

HOME TELEPHONE   MOBILE

E-MAIL

BUSINESS ADDRESS

BUSINESS TELEPHONE   FAX

E-MAIL

WEBSITE

FAMILY DOCTOR   TELEPHONE

BLOOD TYPE   RH   ALLERGIES

IDENTITY CARD NO.

ISSUE DATE   VALID UNTIL

TAX NO.

SOCIAL SECURITY NO.

NATIONAL HEALTH NO.

PASSPORT   VALID UNTIL

ISSUE DATE

VISA   VALID UNTIL

VISA   VALID UNTIL

DRIVING LICENCE   VALID UNTIL

CAR /MOTORCYCLE REGISTRATION NO.

BANK ACCOUNT NO.

CREDIT CARD   VALID UNTIL

HEALTH INSURANCE

TRAVEL INSURANCE

IN CASE OF EMERGENCY, PLEASE CONTACT

PAULO COELHO

SECRETS

2020

Vintage International
Vintage Books
A Division of Penguin Random House LLC
New York

SECRETS

The fruit produces seeds, which transform once again into plants, which again bloom with flowers, which attract the bees, which fertilize the plant and cause it to produce yet more fruit, and so on and so forth until the end of eternity. Greetings, autumn, time to leave behind all that is old, the terrors of the past, and make way for the new.

HIPPIE

2020

JANUARY

S	M	T	W	T	F	S
1			1	2	3	4
2	5	6	7	8	9	10	11
3	12	13	14	15	16	17	18
4	19	20	21	22	23	24	25
5	26	27	28	29	30	31

1 New Year's Day
20 Martin Luther King, Jr. Day

FEBRUARY

S	M	T	W	T	F	S
5						1
6	2	3	4	5	6	7	8
7	9	10	11	12	13	14	15
8	16	17	18	19	20	21	22
9	23	24	25	26	27	28	29

14 Valentine's Day
17 President's Day

MARCH

S	M	T	W	T	F	S
9							
10	1	2	3	4	5	6	7
11	8	9	10	11	12	13	14
12	15	16	17	18	19	20	21
13	22	23	24	25	26	27	28
14	29	30	31

APRIL

S	M	T	W	T	F	S
14				1	2	3	4
15	5	6	7	8	9	10	11
16	12	13	14	15	16	17	18
17	19	20	21	22	23	24	25
18	26	27	28	29	30

10 Good Friday
12 Easter Sunday
13 Easter Monday

MAY

S	M	T	W	T	F	S
18						1	2
19	3	4	5	6	7	8	9
20	10	11	12	13	14	15	16
21	17	18	19	20	21	22	23
22	24	25	26	27	28	29	30
23	31

10 Mother's Day
25 Memorial Day

JUNE

S	M	T	W	T	F	S
23		1	2	3	4	5	6
24	7	8	9	10	11	12	13
25	14	15	16	17	18	19	20
26	21	22	23	24	25	26	27
27	28	29	30

21 Father's day

JULY

S	M	T	W	T	F	S
27				1	2	3	4
28	5	6	7	8	9	10	11
29	12	13	14	15	16	17	18
30	19	20	21	22	23	24	25
31	26	27	28	29	30	31

4 Independence Day

AUGUST

S	M	T	W	T	F	S
31							1
32	2	3	4	5	6	7	8
33	9	10	11	12	13	14	15
34	16	17	18	19	20	21	22
35	23	24	25	26	27	28	29
36	30	31

SEPTEMBER

S	M	T	W	T	F	S
36			1	2	3	4	5
37	6	7	8	9	10	11	12
38	13	14	15	16	17	18	19
39	20	21	22	23	24	25	26
40	27	28	29	30

7 Labor Day

OCTOBER

S	M	T	W	T	F	S
40					1	2	3
41	4	5	6	7	8	9	10
42	11	12	13	14	15	16	17
43	18	19	20	21	22	23	24
44	25	26	27	28	29	30	31

12 Columbus Day

NOVEMBER

S	M	T	W	T	F	S
44							
45	1	2	3	4	5	6	7
46	8	9	10	11	12	13	14
47	15	16	17	18	19	20	21
48	22	23	24	25	26	27	28
49	29	30

3 U.S. Election Day
11 Veteran's Day
26 Thanksgiving Day

DECEMBER

S	M	T	W	T	F	S
49			1	2	3	4	5
50	6	7	8	9	10	11	12
51	13	14	15	16	17	18	19
52	20	21	22	23	24	25	26
53	27	28	29	30	31

25 Christmas Day

2021

JANUARY

S	M	T	W	T	F	S
53					1	2
1	**3**	4	5	6	7	8	9
2	**10**	11	12	13	14	15	16
3	**17**	**18**	19	20	21	22	23
4	**24**	25	26	27	28	29	30
5	**31**					

1 New Year's Day
18 Martin Luther King, Jr. Day

FEBRUARY

S	M	T	W	T	F	S
5		1	2	3	4	5	6
6	**7**	8	9	10	11	12	13
7	**14**	**15**	16	17	18	19	20
8	**21**	22	23	24	25	26	27
9	**28**					

14 Valentine's Day
15 President's Day

MARCH

S	M	T	W	T	F	S
9		1	2	3	4	5	6
10	**7**	8	9	10	11	12	13
11	**14**	15	16	17	18	19	20
12	**21**	22	23	24	25	26	27
13	**28**	29	30	31		

APRIL

S	M	T	W	T	F	S
13					1	**2**	3
14	**4**	**5**	6	7	8	9	10
15	**11**	12	13	14	15	16	17
16	**18**	19	20	21	22	23	24
17	**25**	26	27	28	29	30	

2 Good Friday
4 Easter Sunday
5 Easter Monday

MAY

S	M	T	W	T	F	S
17						1
18	**2**	3	4	5	6	7	8
19	**9**	10	11	12	13	14	15
20	**16**	17	18	19	20	21	22
21	**23**	24	25	26	27	28	29
22	**30**	**31**				

9 Mother's Day
31 Memorial Day

JUNE

S	M	T	W	T	F	S
22		1	2	3	4	5
23	**6**	**7**	8	9	10	11	12
24	**13**	14	15	16	17	18	19
25	**20**	21	22	23	24	25	26
26	**27**	28	29	30		

20 Father's day

JULY

S	M	T	W	T	F	S
26					1	2	3
27	**4**	5	6	7	8	9	10
28	**11**	12	13	14	15	16	17
29	**18**	19	20	21	22	23	24
30	**25**	26	27	28	29	30	31

4 Independence Day

AUGUST

S	M	T	W	T	F	S
31	**1**	2	3	4	5	6	7
32	**8**	9	10	11	12	13	14
33	**15**	16	17	18	19	20	21
34	**22**	23	24	25	26	27	28
35	**29**	30	31			

SEPTEMBER

S	M	T	W	T	F	S
35			1	2	3	4
36	**5**	**6**	7	8	9	10	11
37	**12**	13	14	15	16	17	18
38	**19**	20	21	22	23	24	25
39	**26**	27	28	29	30	

6 Labor Day

OCTOBER

S	M	T	W	T	F	S
39					1	2
40	**3**	4	5	6	7	8	9
41	**10**	11	**12**	13	14	15	16
42	**17**	18	19	20	21	22	23
43	**24**	25	26	27	28	29	30
44	**31**					

12 Columbus Day

NOVEMBER

S	M	T	W	T	F	S
44		1	2	3	4	5	6
45	**7**	8	9	10	**11**	12	13
46	**14**	15	16	17	18	19	20
47	**21**	22	23	24	**25**	26	27
48	**28**	29	30			

11 Veteran's Day
25 Thanksgiving Day

DECEMBER

S	M	T	W	T	F	S
48			1	2	3	4
49	**5**	6	7	8	9	10	11
50	**12**	13	14	15	16	17	18
51	**19**	20	21	22	23	24	25
52	**26**	27	28	29	30	31	

25 Christmas Day

2020 YEAR PLANNER

JANUARY

W	1	
T	2	
F	3	◐
S	4	
S	**5**	
M	6	
T	7	
W	8	
T	9	
F	10	○
S	11	
S	**12**	
M	13	
T	14	
W	15	
T	16	
F	17	◑
S	18	
S	**19**	
M	20	
T	21	
W	22	
T	23	
F	24	●
S	25	
S	**26**	
M	27	
T	28	
W	29	
T	30	
F	31	

FEBRUARY

S	1	
S	**2**	◐
M	3	
T	4	
W	5	
T	6	
F	7	
S	8	
S	**9**	○
M	10	
T	11	
W	12	
T	13	
F	14	
S	15	◐
S	**16**	
M	17	
T	18	
W	19	
T	20	
F	21	
S	22	
S	**23**	●
M	24	
T	25	
W	26	
T	27	
F	28	
S	29	

MARCH

S	**1**	
M	2	◐
T	3	
W	4	
T	5	
F	6	
S	7	
S	**8**	
M	9	○
T	10	
W	11	
T	12	
F	13	
S	14	
S	**15**	
M	16	◑
T	17	
W	18	
T	19	
F	20	
S	21	
S	**22**	
M	23	
T	24	●
W	25	
T	26	
F	27	
S	28	
S	**29**	
M	30	
T	31	

APRIL		
W	1	🌓
T	2	
F	3	
S	4	
S	**5**	
M	6	
T	7	
W	8	○
T	9	
F	10	
S	11	
S	**12**	
M	13	
T	14	
W	15	🌓
T	16	
F	17	
S	18	
S	**19**	
M	20	
T	21	
W	22	
T	23	●
F	24	
S	25	
S	**26**	
M	27	
T	28	
W	29	
T	30	🌓

MAY		
F	1	
S	2	
S	**3**	
M	4	
T	5	
W	6	
T	7	○
F	8	
S	9	
S	**10**	
M	11	
T	12	
W	13	
T	14	🌓
F	15	
S	16	
S	**17**	
M	18	
T	19	
W	20	
T	21	
F	22	●
S	23	
S	**24**	
M	25	
T	26	
W	27	
T	28	
F	29	
S	30	🌓
S	**31**	

JUNE		
M	1	
T	2	
W	3	
T	4	
F	5	○
S	6	
S	**7**	
M	8	
T	9	
W	10	
T	11	
F	12	
S	13	🌓
S	**14**	
M	15	
T	16	
W	17	
T	18	
F	19	
S	20	
S	**21**	●
M	22	
T	23	
W	24	
T	25	
F	26	
S	27	
S	**28**	🌓
M	29	
T	30	

2020 YEAR PLANNER

JULY			AUGUST			SEPTEMBER		
W	1		S	1		T	1	
T	2		S	**2**		W	2	○
F	3		M	3	○	T	3	
S	4		T	4		F	4	
S	**5**	○	W	5		S	5	
M	6		T	6		S	**6**	
T	7		F	7		M	7	
W	8		S	8		T	8	
T	9		S	**9**		W	9	
F	10		M	10		T	10	◑
S	11		T	11	◑	F	11	
S	**12**		W	12		S	12	
M	13	◑	T	13		S	**13**	
T	14		F	14		M	14	
W	15		S	15		T	15	
T	16		S	**16**		W	16	
F	17		M	17		T	17	●
S	18		T	18		F	18	
S	**19**		W	19	●	S	19	
M	20	●	T	20		S	**20**	
T	21		F	21		M	21	
W	22		S	22		T	22	
T	23		S	**23**		W	23	
F	24		M	24		T	24	◐
S	25		T	25	◐	F	25	
S	**26**		W	26		S	26	
M	27	◐	T	27		S	**27**	
T	28		F	28		M	28	
W	29		S	29		T	29	
T	30		S	**30**		W	30	
F	31		M	31				

OCTOBER

T	1	○
F	2	
S	3	
S	**4**	
M	5	
T	6	
W	7	
T	8	
F	9	
S	10	◑
S	**11**	
M	12	
T	13	
W	14	
T	15	
F	16	●
S	17	
S	**18**	
M	19	
T	20	
W	21	
T	22	
F	23	◐
S	24	
S	**25**	
M	26	
T	27	
W	28	
T	29	
F	30	
S	31	○

NOVEMBER

S	**1**	
M	2	
T	3	
W	4	
T	5	
F	6	
S	7	
S	8	◑
M	9	
T	10	
W	11	
T	12	
F	13	
S	14	
S	15	●
M	16	
T	17	
W	18	
T	19	
F	20	
S	21	
S	22	◐
M	23	
T	24	
W	25	
T	26	
F	27	
S	28	
S	**29**	
M	30	○

DECEMBER

T	1	
W	2	
T	3	
F	4	
S	5	
S	**6**	
M	7	
T	8	◑
W	9	
T	10	
F	11	
S	12	
S	**13**	
M	14	●
T	15	
W	16	
T	17	
F	18	
S	19	
S	**20**	
M	21	
T	22	◐
W	23	
T	24	
F	25	
S	26	
S	**27**	
M	28	
T	29	
W	30	○
T	31	

JANUARY

Communion

Energy is to be found in the tiniest things man encounters in his path; the world is the true classroom, the Love Supreme knows you are alive and will teach you all you need to know.

HIPPIE

1 Wednesday

2 Thursday

Only someone who listens to the noise
of the present can make the right decision.

THE PILGRIMAGE

3 Friday

4 Saturday

Love does not need to be understood.
It needs only to be shown.

MANUSCRIPT FOUND IN ACCRA

5 | Sunday

6 | Monday

7 | Tuesday

8 Wednesday

9 Thursday

I don't know if love appears suddenly – but I know
that I'm open to love, ready for love.

BRIDA

10 | Friday

11 | Saturday

Once their hearts had said everything, they began
to share the great mysteries.

BY THE RIVER PIEDRA I SAT DOWN AND WEPT

12 Sunday

13 | Monday

14 | Tuesday

15 Wednesday

16 Thursday

If you're alive, you should wave your arms about,
leap in the air, make noise, laugh and talk
to people, because life is the exact opposite
of death.

CHRONICLE – FRAGMENTS OF A DIARY

17 Friday

18 Saturday

Like love, for example. People either feel
it or they don't, and there isn't a force in the world
that can make them feel it.

THE WITCH OF PORTOBELLO

19 Sunday

20 | Monday

21 | Tuesday

22 Wednesday

23 Thursday

What does it mean to love someone?
It means remaining free, so that the person
by your side never feels enslaved by your love.

HIPPIE

24 Friday

25 Saturday

It's the willingness to believe life is a miracle
that allows miracles to happen.

CHRONICLE – TWENTY YEARS ON

26 Sunday

27 Monday

10 Minutes of Morning

Tennis ?

28 Tuesday

10 Morning Minutes

PickelBall

29 Wednesday

W Morning Minutes

Pixer

30 Thursday

W Morning Minutes

Peter Jill

To love is to commune with another human being
and discover God's spark in that other person.

BY THE RIVER PIEDRA I SAT DOWN AND WEPT

31 Friday

W Morning Minute

Jill,

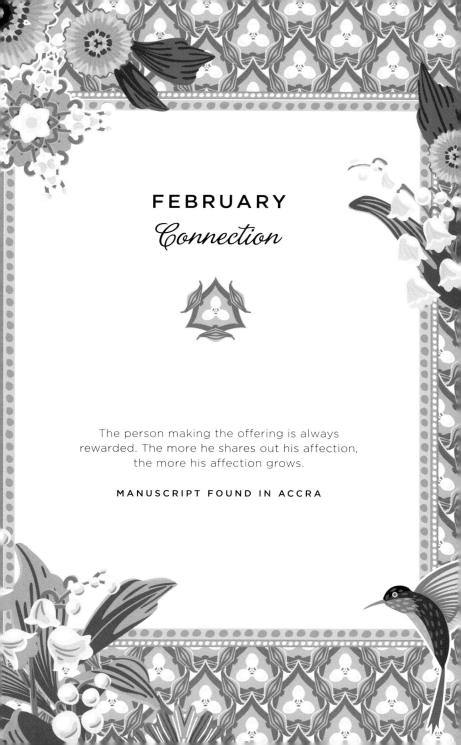

FEBRUARY

Connection

The person making the offering is always
rewarded. The more he shares out his affection,
the more his affection grows.

MANUSCRIPT FOUND IN ACCRA

1 Saturday

2 Sunday

The future is unreliable because it is guided
by decisions made in the here and now.

THE WITCH OF PORTOBELLO

3 Monday

4 Tuesday

Love doesn't limit,
it broadens our horizons.

CHRONICLE – IN THE CORNERS OF THE HEART

5 Wednesday

6 Thursday

7 | Friday

8 | Saturday

9 Sunday

Happiness lies in the heart of the person fighting,
because he or she cares nothing about
victory or defeat; all that matters is fighting
the Good Fight.

T H E   P I L G R I M A G E

10 Monday

11 Tuesday

A warrior of light shares his world with the people
he loves. He tries to encourage them to do
the things they would like to do.

CHRONICLE – WARRIOR OF LIGHT

12 Wednesday

13 Thursday

14 | Friday

15 | Saturday

16 | Sunday

Don't be alone in the search, because if you take
a wrong step, you'll have no one there to help
put you right.

THE WITCH OF PORTOBELLO

17 Monday

18 Tuesday

There's no point in understanding the entire
Universe if you're alone.

BRIDA

19 Wednesday

20 Thursday

21 Friday

22 Saturday

23 Sunday

A sense of gratitude is important; no one gets
very far if he forgets those who were with him
in his hour of need.

THE WINNER STANDS ALONE

24 Monday

25 Tuesday

We only understand life and the Universe
when we find our Soulmate.

BRIDA

26 | Wednesday

27 | Thursday

28 Friday

29 Saturday

Those who make promises they don't keep end up
powerless and frustrated; the same happens with
those who cling to the promises they made.

THE DEVIL AND MISS PRYM

MARCH

Giving

Suffering occurs when we want other people to love us in the way we imagine we want to be loved, and not in the way that love should manifest itself – free and untrammelled, guiding us with its force and driving us on.

THE ZAHIR

1 Sunday

You can only learn when you teach.

THE PILGRIMAGE

2 Monday

3 Tuesday

It takes courage for us to change our mind
when we realize that we are merely the
instruments of His will, and it is His will that
we should follow.

HIPPIE

4 Wednesday

5 Thursday

6 | Friday

7 | Saturday

8 | Sunday

Lord, always give us enthusiasm,
because enthusiasm is a way of praying.

CHRONICLE – THE PRAYER I FORGOT

9 Monday

10 Tuesday

I know that people in love end up transmitting
their love to the world in which they live.

THE WITCH OF PORTOBELLO

11 Wednesday

12 Thursday

13 | Friday

14 | Saturday

15 | Sunday

Like the sun, life spreads its light
in all directions.

MANUSCRIPT FOUND IN ACCRA

16 Monday

17 Tuesday

If we're tolerant of others, it's easier to accept our
own mistakes. Then, without guilt or bitterness,
we can improve our attitude towards life.

CHRONICLE – STORIES ABOUT FORGIVENESS

18 | Wednesday

19 | Thursday

20 Friday

21 Saturday

22 | Sunday

The soul likes deep,
beautiful things.

THE WINNER STANDS ALONE

23 Monday

24 Tuesday

The simplest things in life are the most
extraordinary. Let them reveal themselves.

MANUSCRIPT FOUND IN ACCRA

25 | Wednesday

26 | Thursday

27 Friday

28 Saturday

29 Sunday

There is nothing worse than being punished
for something you didn't do.

H I P P I E

30 Monday

31 Tuesday

He never forgets his friends, for their blood
mingled with his on the battlefield.

MANUAL OF THE WARRIOR OF LIGHT

APRIL

Sharing

A warrior of light tries to establish what
he can truly rely on. And he always checks
that he carries three things with him:
faith, hope and love.

MANUAL OF THE WARRIOR OF LIGHT

1 Wednesday

2 Thursday

Love is free and is not ruled
by our will or by what we do.

MANUSCRIPT FOUND IN ACCRA

3 Friday

4 Saturday

Remember the good things you have done.
They will give you courage.

THE FIFTH MOUNTAIN

5 | Sunday

6 | Monday

7 | Tuesday

8 Wednesday

9 Thursday

Love – it's impossible to conceive
of a life without love.

HIPPIE

10 Friday

11 Saturday

Happiness is something that multiplies
when shared.

BY THE RIVER PIEDRA I SAT DOWN AND WEPT

12 Sunday

13 | Monday

14 | Tuesday

15 Wednesday

16 Thursday

Seek out people who aren't afraid of making
mistakes and who, therefore, do make mistakes.
They are precisely the kind of people who
change the world.

ALEPH

17 Friday

18 Saturday

Help us to be humble when we receive
and joyful when we give.

MANUSCRIPT FOUND IN ACCRA

19 Sunday

20 | Monday

21 | Tuesday

22 Wednesday

23 Thursday

In order to learn,
you must be humble.

BRIDA

24 Friday

25 Saturday

Only cowards hide behind silence.

THE DEVIL AND MISS PRYM

26 | Sunday

27 Monday

28 Tuesday

29 | Wednesday

30 | Thursday

When we have a goal in life, it can be for
better or worse, depending on the path we take
in order to achieve it, and the way in which
we walk that path.

THE PILGRIMAGE

MAY

Insight

But how does God's Love manifest itself?
Through the Love of man.

ADULTERY

1 Friday

2 Saturday

3 | Sunday

The worst of all murders
is the one that kills our joy for life.

HIPPIE

4 Monday

5 Tuesday

It's all a matter of knowing
when to stop.

ALEPH

6 | Wednesday

7 | Thursday

8 Friday

9 Saturday

10 Sunday

It's enough to know that the fundamental
questions of life will never be answered,
and that we can, nevertheless, still go forward.

THE ZAHIR

11 Monday

12 Tuesday

Help us to awaken the Love sleeping within
us before we awaken love in other people.
Only then will we be able to attract affection,
enthusiasm and respect.

M A N U S C R I P T   F O U N D   I N   A C C R A

13 Wednesday

14 Thursday

15 Friday

16 Saturday

17 | Sunday

It isn't explanations that carry
us forward, it's our will to go on.

B R I D A

18 Monday

19 Tuesday

Dare to dream, and you will be doing what you
can to transform that dream into reality.

THE PILGRIMAGE

20 Wednesday

21 Thursday

22 Friday

23 Saturday

24 | Sunday

The ways in which fate changes people are always
favourable if we know how to decipher them.

THE WITCH OF PORTOBELLO

25 Monday

26 Tuesday

Pain means nothing compared to the joy
of having done my duty.

THE FIFTH MOUNTAIN

27 Wednesday

28 Thursday

29 Friday

30 Saturday

31 Sunday

Only one thing makes a dream impossible,
and that is the fear of failure.

THE ALCHEMIST

JUNE

Revelation

Their unconfessed sentiments had yet
to be revealed, but they would not
remain unknown for long.

HIPPIE

1 Monday

2 Tuesday

Love is always new.

BY THE RIVER PIEDRA I SAT DOWN AND WEPT

3 | Wednesday

4 | Thursday

5 Friday

6 Saturday

7 Sunday

When our hearts are weary, we can still carry on
thanks to the strength of our Faith.

MANUSCRIPT FOUND IN ACCRA

8 Monday

9 Tuesday

We only really understand the miracle of life
when we allow the unexpected to happen.

BY THE RIVER PIEDRA I SAT DOWN AND WEPT

10 | Wednesday

11 | Thursday

12 Friday

13 Saturday

14 | Sunday

Love is capable of transforming a person,
that is how I discovered who I was.

THE WINNER STANDS ALONE

15 Monday

16 Tuesday

God manifests himself in everything,
but the word is one of his most favoured
methods of doing so.

BRIDA

17 | Wednesday

18 | Thursday

19 Friday

20 Saturday

21 | Sunday

No one knows why the current took them
to that particular island and not to the one
they wanted to reach.

THE ZAHIR

22 Monday

23 Tuesday

Good and Evil have the same face,
it all depends on when they cross the path
of each human being.

THE DEVIL AND MISS PRYM

24 Wednesday

25 Thursday

26 Friday

27 Saturday

28 | Sunday

What does learning mean: accumulating
knowledge or transforming your life?

THE WITCH OF PORTOBELLO

29 Monday

30 Tuesday

There are still many things I haven't seen or
experienced. Where will my heart go, if I don't yet
know all the many possible roads?

HIPPIE

JULY
Solitude

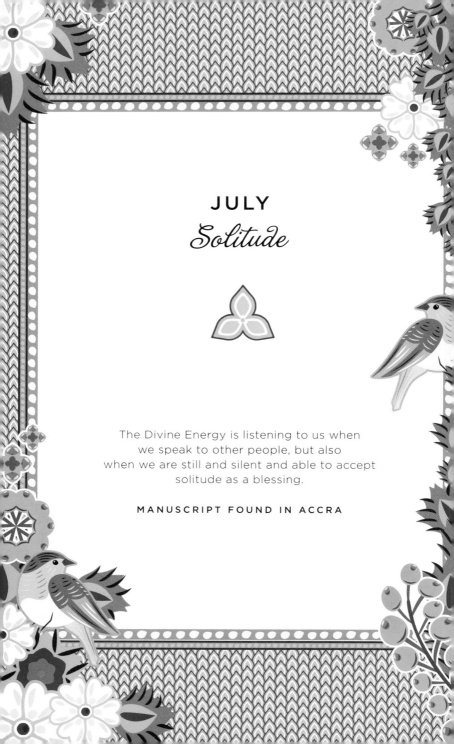

The Divine Energy is listening to us when
we speak to other people, but also
when we are still and silent and able to accept
solitude as a blessing.

MANUSCRIPT FOUND IN ACCRA

1 Wednesday

2 Thursday

Everything has to be a personal manifestation
of our will to win the Good Fight. Otherwise, if we
fail to understand that we need everyone and
everything, we will become arrogant warriors.

THE PILGRIMAGE

3 Friday

4 Saturday

I know which door I need to open, even though
it's concealed amongst many other entrances and
exits. All I need is a little silence.

THE WITCH OF PORTOBELLO

5 | Sunday

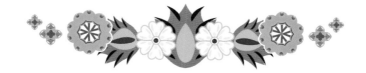

6 Monday

7 Tuesday

8 Wednesday

9 Thursday

We each have our own way of looking at life and
of coping with difficulties and with conquests.

THE PILGRIMAGE

10 Friday

11 Saturday

If we sit in silence for an hour, we will begin to
hear God, but if we shout for joy, God will also
hear us and come to bless us.

HIPPIE

12 | Sunday

13 Monday

14 Tuesday

15 Wednesday

16 Thursday

The meaning of my life was the one
I chose to give to it.

THE FIFTH MOUNTAIN

17 Friday

18 Saturday

I need to enjoy all the graces God gave me today.
Grace cannot be squirreled away.

CHRONICLE – BETWEEN EKATERINBURG AND NOVOSIBIRSK

19 Sunday

20 Monday

21 Tuesday

22 Wednesday

23 Thursday

All you have to do is pay attention; lessons always arrive when you are ready, and if you can read the signs, you will learn everything you need to know in order to take the next step.

THE ZAHIR

24 Friday

25 Saturday

Blessed be those who
do not fear solitude.

MANUSCRIPT FOUND IN ACCRA

26 | Sunday

27 Monday

28 Tuesday

29 Wednesday

30 Thursday

The warrior takes responsibility for everything
he does, even if he has to pay a high price
for his mistake.

MANUAL OF THE WARRIOR OF LIGHT

31 | Friday

Help us to understand, that there are certain
things so important, that we have to discover
them, without anyone's help.

MANUSCRIPT FOUND IN ACCRA

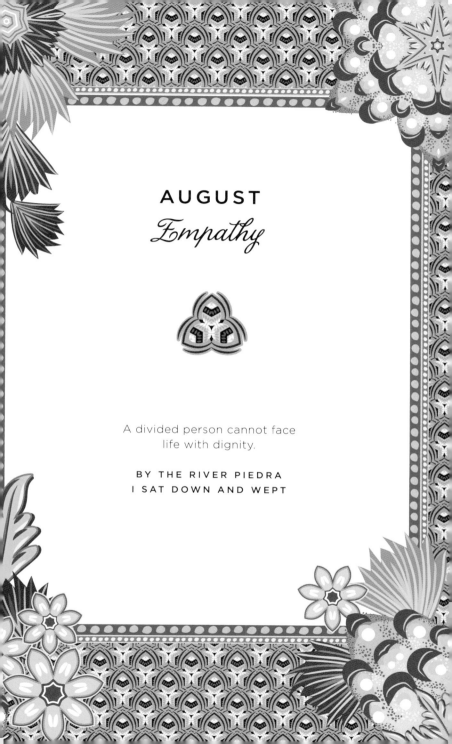

AUGUST

Empathy

A divided person cannot face
life with dignity.

**BY THE RIVER PIEDRA
I SAT DOWN AND WEPT**

1 Saturday

Beauty exists not in sameness,
but in difference.

MANUSCRIPT FOUND IN ACCRA

2 Sunday

3 Monday

4 Tuesday

5 Wednesday

6 Thursday

Where there is joy after tragedy, there will always
be an example to be followed.

CHRONICLE – AT THE END OF THE DARK TUNNEL

7 | Friday

8 | Saturday

Many are the emotions that stir the human
heart when it decides to set off along the spiritual
path. It could be something noble, like faith, love
for one's fellow man or charity. Or it could be
merely a whim, fear of loneliness, curiosity
or a desire to be loved.

HIPPIE

9 Sunday

10 | Monday

11 | Tuesday

12 Wednesday

13 Thursday

A warrior of light is in the world in order
to help his fellow man and not in order to
condemn his neighbor.

MANUAL OF THE WARRIOR OF LIGHT

14 Friday

15 Saturday

Whenever we welcome someone, we open
ourselves to adventure and mystery.

MAKTUB – THE TRADITION OF WELCOMING OTHERS

16 Sunday

17 Monday

18 Tuesday

19 | Wednesday

20 | Thursday

Receiving is also an act of love. Allowing someone
else to make us happy will make them happy too.

M A N U S C R I P T   F O U N D   I N   A C C R A

21 Friday

22 Saturday

Our true friends are those who are with
us when the good things happen.

THE ZAHIR

23 | Sunday

24 Monday

25 Tuesday

26 Wednesday

27 Thursday

People who seek only success rarely find it,
because success is not an end in itself,
but a consequence.

MANUSCRIPT FOUND IN ACCRA

28 Friday

29 Saturday

The path to knowledge is open to everyone,
to ordinary people.

THE PILGRIMAGE

30 | Sunday

31 Monday

That was true love, a question
for which there is no answer.

HIPPIE

SEPTEMBER

Understanding

When faced by any loss, there's no point
in trying to recover what has been, it's best to
take advantage of the large space that opens
up before us and fill it with something new.

ALEPH

1 Tuesday

Everything is permitted,
except interrupting a manifestation of love.

THE PILGRIMAGE

2 Wednesday

3 Thursday

4 Friday

5 Saturday

6 Sunday

We must be conscious of death if we are
to have a proper understanding of life.

THE WINNER STANDS ALONE

7 Monday

8 Tuesday

Anyone who loves must know how to lose
himself and find himself again.

BY THE RIVER PIEDRA I SAT DOWN AND WEPT

9 Wednesday

10 Thursday

11 Friday

12 Saturday

13 Sunday

You can only know a good wine
if you have first tasted a bad one.

BRIDA

14 Monday

15 Tuesday

Fear of suffering is worse
than the actual suffering.

THE ALCHEMIST

16 Wednesday

17 Thursday

18 Friday

19 Saturday

20 | Sunday

Anyone who loves in the expectation
of receiving some reward is wasting her time.

THE DEVIL AND MISS PRYM

21 Monday

22 Tuesday

Success does not come from having one's
work recognized by others. It is the fruit of a seed
that you lovingly planted.

MANUSCRIPT FOUND IN ACCRA

23 Wednesday

24 Thursday

25 Friday

26 Saturday

27 | Sunday

The Lord hears the prayers of those who ask to be
able to forget hatred, but is deaf to those who
wish to run away from love.

THE FIFTH MOUNTAIN

28 Monday

29 Tuesday

Forgiveness is a very difficult art.

HIPPIE

30 Wednesday

OCTOBER

Determination

When someone makes a decision, he is really
diving into a strong current that will carry him
to places he had never dreamed of when
he first made the decision.

THE ALCHEMIST

1 Thursday

What is a life without love?
It's the tree that gives no fruit.

HIPPIE

2 Friday

3 Saturday

You are merely a warrior of light. There is no
reason to feel proud or to feel guilty, only
a reason to fulfill your destiny.

CHRONICLE – THE WARRIOR OF LIGHT AND HIS WORLD

4 Sunday

5 Monday

6 Tuesday

7 Wednesday

8 Thursday

The great wisdom of life is to realize that we can
be the masters of the things that try to enslave us.

MANUSCRIPT FOUND IN ACCRA

9 Friday

10 Saturday

How can we do the impossible?
With enthusiasm.

THE FIFTH MOUNTAIN

11 Sunday

12 Monday

13 Tuesday

14 Wednesday

15 Thursday

The decisions he made required courage,
a degree of detachment, and, at times, even a
little madness, not the kind of madness that
destroys, but the sort that carries a person
beyond his own limits.

THE WINNER STANDS ALONE

16 Friday

17 Saturday

If you're not content with your lot,
then risk changing everything and devoting
yourself to what you love.

CHRONICLE – RESPECTING WORK

18 Sunday

19 Monday

20 Tuesday

21 Wednesday

22 Thursday

The human spirit feeds on mysteries. It flees
routine. It tries the new, the spectacular.

MAKTUB – MYSTERIES

23 Friday

24 Saturday

It's not hard to rebuild a life. It's enough to know
that we are as strong as we were before and
to put this strength to good use.

THE FIFTH MOUNTAIN

25 | Sunday

26 Monday

27 Tuesday

28 Wednesday

29 Thursday

For those who want to cross thresholds,
the doors are always open. You just have
to turn the handle.

HIPPIE

30 Friday

31 Saturday

When you want something, the universe
conspires in helping you to achieve it.

THE ALCHEMIST

NOVEMBER

Trust

The aim of everything I've looked for in my life—allowing love to manifest itself in me without barriers, letting it fill up my blank spaces, making me dance, smile, justify my life.

THE WITCH OF PORTOBELLO

1 Sunday

Excessive caution destroys the soul and the heart,
because living is an act of courage.

MANUSCRIPT FOUND IN ACCRA

2 Monday

3 Tuesday

4 Wednesday

5 Thursday

6 Friday

7 Saturday

8 | Sunday

A part of my heart was telling me that I was being
rewarded because I hadn't given up, I made a
choice, and I fought to the end.

THE WINNER STANDS ALONE

9 Monday

10 Tuesday

Love isn't desire or knowledge or admiration.
It's a challenge, it's an invisible fire.

THE WITCH OF PORTOBELLO

11 Wednesday

---

12 Thursday

13 | Friday

14 | Saturday

15 Sunday

The Universe always conspires
to help dreamers.

BY THE RIVER PIEDRA I SAT DOWN AND WEPT

16 Monday

17 Tuesday

The closer you get to your dream,
the more your Personal Legend becomes
your real reason for living.

THE ALCHEMIST

18 | Wednesday

19 | Thursday

20 Friday

21 Saturday

22 | Sunday

Concentrate only on the moments when you
achieved what you desired, and that strength will
help you to achieve what you want.

THE FIFTH MOUNTAIN

23 | Monday

24 | Tuesday

Having the courage to take the steps we always
wanted to take is the only way of showing
that we trust in God.

BRIDA

25 Wednesday

26 Thursday

27 Friday

28 Saturday

When things happen without planning or
anticipation, they turn out to be more enjoyable
and more profitable too.

HIPPIE

29 | Sunday

30 | Monday

Revisiting the past is no use, it serves only
to place figurative shackles on our feet and
remove any sign of hope in humanity.

HIPPIE

DECEMBER

Preservation

We don't choose the things
that happen to us, but we can choose
how we react to them.

HIPPIE

1 | Tuesday

Remember always to know
what you want.

THE ALCHEMIST

2 | Wednesday

3 | Thursday

4 Friday

5 Saturday

6 | Sunday

We only discover that a plan is wrong
when we take it to its ultimate consequences,
or when all-merciful God leads us in
another direction.

THE WINNER STANDS ALONE

7 | Monday

8 | Tuesday

If we succeed in understanding the sacred
harmony of our daily life, we will always be
on the right path, because our daily tasks
are also our divine tasks.

CHRONICLE – CONVERSATIONS WITH THE MASTER

9 Wednesday

10 Thursday

11 Friday

12 Saturday

13 | Sunday

It's important to let certain things go.
To release them. To cut loose.

THE ZAHIR

14 Monday

15 Tuesday

Love cannot be held prisoner because
it is a river and will overflow its banks.

THE WITCH OF PORTOBELLO

16 Wednesday

17 Thursday

18 | Friday

19 | Saturday

20 | Sunday

You will only be loved and respected
if you love and respect yourself.

MANUSCRIPT FOUND IN ACCRA

21 Monday

22 Tuesday

A warrior never picks
the fruit while it is still green.

MANUAL OF THE WARRIOR OF LIGHT

23 | Wednesday

24 | Thursday

25 Friday

26 Saturday

27 | Sunday

You were obviously not great enough
if you could abandon your dream just because
of what some stranger said.

CHRONICLE – READER'S STORIES

28 Monday

29 Tuesday

The only way to make the right decision
is by knowing what would be the wrong decision.
And then decide.

THE PILGRIMAGE

30 Wednesday

31 Thursday

Original title: *Segredos 2020*

Copyright © 2019 Paulo Coelho and Mosaikk AS
http://paulocoelhoblog.com/

Published by arrangement with Sant Jordi Asociados, Agencia Literaria, S.L.U.,
Barcelona (Spain). www.santjordi-asociados.com

Vintage ISBN: 978-1-9848-9812-8

Quote selection: Márcia Botelho
Translation copyright © Margaret Jull Costa
Illustrations by Catalina Estrada, www.catalinaestrada.com
Author photograph © Paul Macleod
Design by Lene Stangebye Geving / Mireia Barreras

www.vintagebooks.com

Printed and bound by TBB, a. s., Slovakia, 2019

First Vintage International edition: August 2019